TRIATHLON

 AN INSPIRATION

ALI CLARKE

summersdale

TRIATHLON

Summersdale Publishers Ltd
46 West Street
Chichester
West Sussex
PO19 1RP
UK

www.summersdale.com

Printed and bound in China

ISBN: 978-1-84953-616-5

Substantial discounts on bulk quantities of Summersdale books are available to corporations, professional associations and other organisations. For details contact Nicky Douglas by telephone: +44 (0) 1243 756902, fax: +44 (0) 1243 786300 or email: nicky@summersdale.com.

INTRODUCTION

Train harder. Sweat more. Be faster. Not just the lyrics of a triathlete's life, but the rhyme, rhythm and soul. Because a triathlon is not just a one-off race where you train two weeks prior to the event – a triathlon is a lifestyle you choose: one that you eat, sleep and breathe, day in day out. It's all or nothing.

Competing in a triathlon is hard. But training for a triathlon is harder still: it is one of the toughest things you will do in your life. The physical effort is gruelling, but it's the mental effort – the motivation, determination and commitment – that will be the controlling factor of your achievement. As a triathlete there's no room for quitters, no room for fair-weather mentality. Whatever the weather, whatever your physical or mental state, nothing should be able to deter you from leaving your comfort zone to go to a place where you'll be tested at all levels.

But, realistically, everyone – even if you're a relentless professional – will have times when your resolve is challenged and you're struggling to commit. That's where this book will be your conduit and go-to. So flick through these pages filled with inspirational photos, quotes and mantras and let them fire you with the willpower and encouragement you need to continue. Once you reach that finishing line and feel the adrenaline and endorphins rush through your body, you'll know that it was worth the pain… And then you'll want to do it all over again.

Swim. Bike. Run.

EVERY ACCOMPLISHMENT
—— STARTS WITH THE ——
DECISION TO TRY.

RACING IS PAIN, AND THAT'S WHY YOU DO IT, TO CHALLENGE YOURSELF AND THE LIMITS OF YOUR PHYSICAL AND MENTAL BARRIERS.

MARK ALLEN

IF YOU TRAIN YOUR MIND
FOR RUNNING, EVERYTHING
ELSE WILL BE EASY.

AMBY BURFOOT

ONE THING WE CAN ALL CONTROL IS EFFORT. MARK CUBAN

THOSE WHO DON'T JUMP WILL NEVER FLY.

LEENA AHMAD ALMASHAT

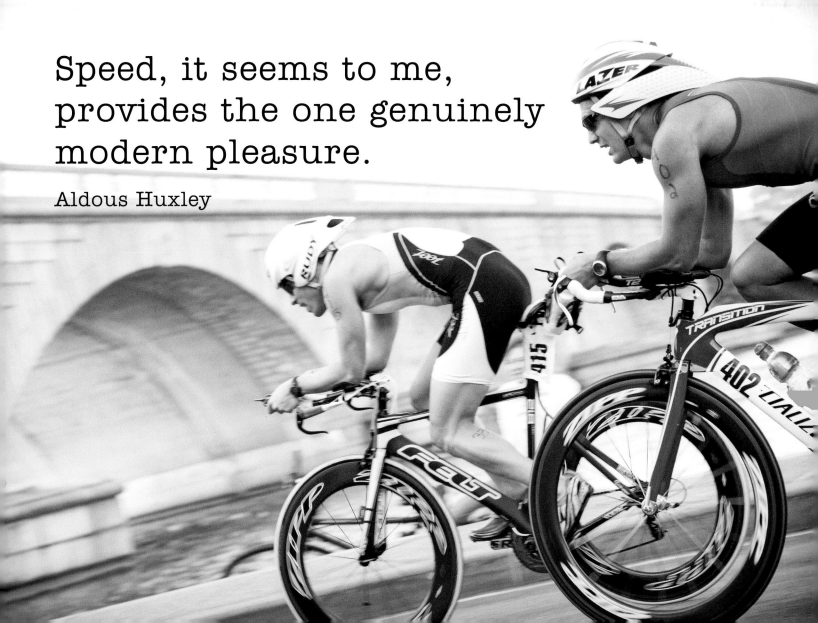

Speed, it seems to me, provides the one genuinely modern pleasure.

Aldous Huxley

YOU HAVE TO GO WHOLEHEARTEDLY
INTO ANYTHING IN ORDER TO ACHIEVE
ANYTHING WORTH HAVING.

FRANK LLOYD WRIGHT

WHEN YOU WANT TO SUCCEED AS
BAD AS YOU WANT TO BREATHE,
THEN YOU WILL BE SUCCESSFUL.

ERIC THOMAS

IT ALWAYS SEEMS
IMPOSSIBLE UNTIL
IT'S **DONE.**

NELSON MANDELA

NEVER GIVE UP ON SOMETHING

YOU REALLY WANT.

GOALS ARE THE FUEL IN THE FURNACE OF ACHIEVEMENT.

BRIAN TRACEY

WINNERS NEVER QUIT AND
QUITTERS NEVER WIN.

VINCE LOMBARDI

PHYSICAL CHANGE STARTS WITH **MENTAL** CHANGE.

IT'S THE LITTLE DETAILS THAT
ARE VITAL. LITTLE THINGS
MAKE BIG THINGS HAPPEN.

JOHN WOODEN

THE WILL TO WIN MEANS
NOTHING IF YOU HAVEN'T
THE WILL TO PREPARE.

Juma Ikangaa

SOMETIMES YOU HAVE TO TAKE THE BULL BY THE HORNS.

Proverb

WHEN PAIN COMES YOU KNOW
WHAT I DO? I SMILE.

CHRIS McCORMACK

IN RUNNING, IT DOESN'T MATTER
WHETHER YOU COME IN FIRST,
IN THE MIDDLE OF THE PACK,
OR LAST. YOU CAN SAY, 'I HAVE
FINISHED.' THERE IS A LOT OF
SATISFACTION IN THAT.

FRED LEBOW

NOBODY SAID IT WOULD BE EASY,
THEY SAID IT WOULD BE WORTH IT.

IT'S HARD TO BEAT A PERSON
WHO NEVER GIVES UP.

BABE RUTH

NOTHING GREAT WAS EVER
ACHIEVED WITHOUT ENTHUSIASM.

RALPH WALDO EMERSON

DON'T WISH

── FOR IT. ──

WORK FOR IT.

BE BOLD WHEN OTHERS ARE SCARED.

THOMAS J. POWELL

MAKE TIME FOR IT. JUST GET IT DONE. NOBODY EVER GOT STRONG OR GOT IN SHAPE BY THINKING ABOUT IT. THEY DID IT.

JIM WENDLER

IF IT DOESN'T CHALLENGE YOU,
IT DOESN'T CHANGE YOU.

FRED DEVITO

TRAINING IN THE COMPANY
—— OF OTHERS IS ALWAYS ——
THE MOST REWARDING.

THE ULTIMATE GOAL
—— IS DOING YOUR BEST ——
AND ENJOYING IT.

The difference
between 'try'
and 'triumph' is
a little 'umph'.

Marvin Phillips

SUCCESS IS NOT FINAL, FAILURE IS NOT FATAL: IT IS THE COURAGE TO CONTINUE THAT COUNTS.

ANONYMOUS

IT'S ALL ABOUT HOW HARD YOU TRI!

STAMINA, SPEED, STRENGTH, SKILL AND SPIRIT – BUT THE GREATEST OF THESE IS SPIRIT.

KEN DOHERTY

THERE IS ONLY ONE PERFECT
ROAD, AND THAT ROAD IS AHEAD
OF YOU, ALWAYS AHEAD OF YOU.

SRI CHINMOY

RUNNING IS LIKE MOUTHWASH:
IF YOU CAN FEEL THE BURN
IT'S WORKING.

BRIAN TACKETT

THE VALUE OF ACHIEVEMENT **LIES IN ACHIEVING**.

ALBERT EINSTEIN

THE OPEN ROAD IS A BECKONING...
A PLACE WHERE A MAN CAN
LOSE HIMSELF.

WILLIAM LEAST HEAT-MOON

DON'T STOP WHEN YOU ARE TIRED;

———— STOP WHEN ————

YOU ARE FINISHED.

FOCUS ON HOW FAR
—— YOU'VE COME; NOT HOW FAR ——
YOU'VE GOT TO GO.

IT HURTS.
BECAUSE IT
MATTERED.
JOHN GREEN

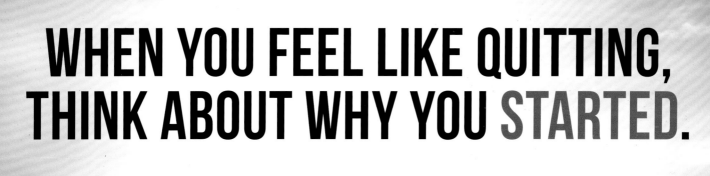

WHEN YOU FEEL LIKE QUITTING, THINK ABOUT WHY YOU STARTED.

YOU CAN'T PUT A LIMIT ON ANYTHING.

MICHAEL PHELPS

Optimism is the faith that leads to achievement.

Helen Keller

EVERY TIME I GO OUT AND
RACE IT'S A GOAL TO GO OUT
AND RUN FASTER THAN I'VE
EVER DONE BEFORE.

PAULA RADCLIFFE

AT FIRST YOU
FEEL LIKE
DYING,

THEN YOU FEEL
REBORN.

IT'S NOT ABOUT FINDING YOUR LIMITS. —— IT'S ABOUT FINDING OUT WHAT LIES —— JUST BEYOND THEM.

DISCIPLINE IS CHOOSING BETWEEN —— WHAT YOU WANT NOW AND —— WHAT YOU WANT MOST.

THE MIRACLE ISN'T THAT I
FINISHED. THE MIRACLE IS THAT
I HAD THE COURAGE TO START.

JOHN BINGHAM

Four wheels move the body.
TWO WHEELS MOVE THE SOUL.

PERSISTENCE CAN CHANGE FAILURE INTO EXTRAORDINARY ACHIEVEMENT.

MATT BIONDI

IF YOU AREN'T GOING ALL THE WAY,
WHY GO AT ALL?

JOE NAMATH

WE ARE JUDGED BY
—— WHAT WE FINISH, ——
NOT BY WHAT WE START.

DON'T LET FATIGUE MAKE A COWARD OF YOU.

STEVE PREFONTAINE

PUSH YOURSELF

—— A BIT ——

HARDER.

A **TRIATHLETE** IS A PERSON WHO DOESN'T UNDERSTAND
THAT ONE SPORT IS HARD ENOUGH.

IT'S WHEN THE DISCOMFORT
STRIKES THAT ONE REALISES
A STRONG MIND IS THE MOST
POWERFUL WEAPON OF ALL.

CHRISSIE WELLINGTON

IT IS THE UNKNOWN AROUND
THE CORNER THAT TURNS
MY WHEELS.

HEINZ STÜCKE

SPECTACULAR ACHIEVEMENT
IS ALWAYS PRECEDED BY
UNSPECTACULAR PREPARATION.

ROBERT H. SCHULLER

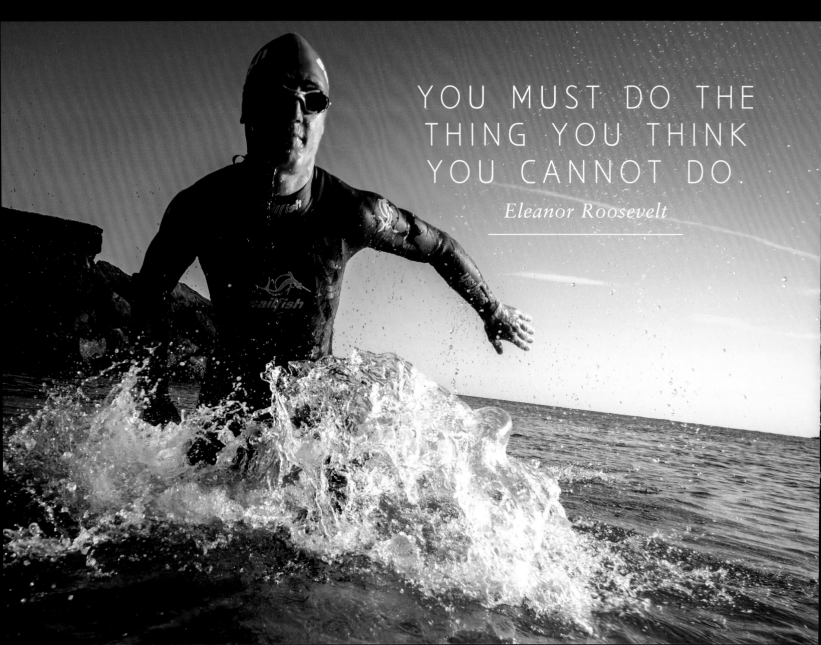

DON'T LOSE FAITH,
YOU'VE GOT THIS.

NEVER GIVE UP ON A DREAM JUST BECAUSE OF THE TIME IT WILL TAKE TO ACCOMPLISH IT. THE TIME WILL PASS ANYWAY.

Earl Nightingale

FORM AND FUNCTION
SHOULD BE ONE.

FRANK LLOYD WRIGHT

TRAINING IN THE RAIN, WIND AND COLD
—— ISN'T EASY, BUT DOING IT WILL ——
MAKE YOU STRONGER.

I **TRI** THEREFORE I AM.

ABILITY IS WHAT YOU'RE
CAPABLE OF DOING. MOTIVATION
DETERMINES WHAT YOU DO.
ATTITUDE DETERMINES HOW
WELL YOU DO IT.

LOU HOLTZ

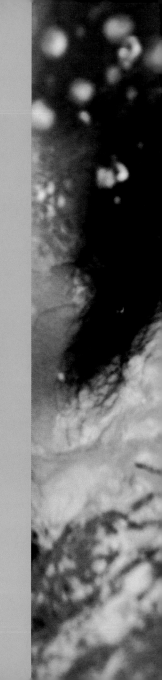

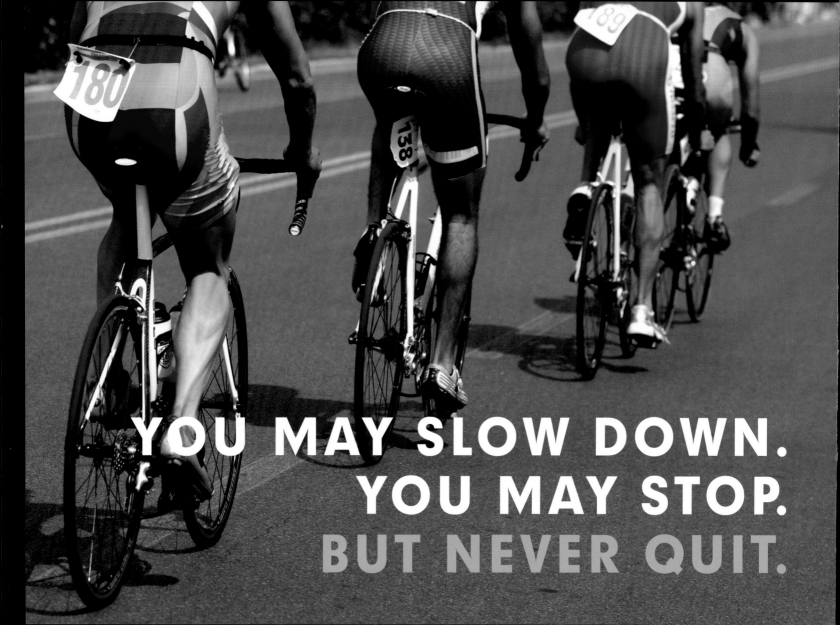

YOU MAY SLOW DOWN.
YOU MAY STOP.
BUT NEVER QUIT.

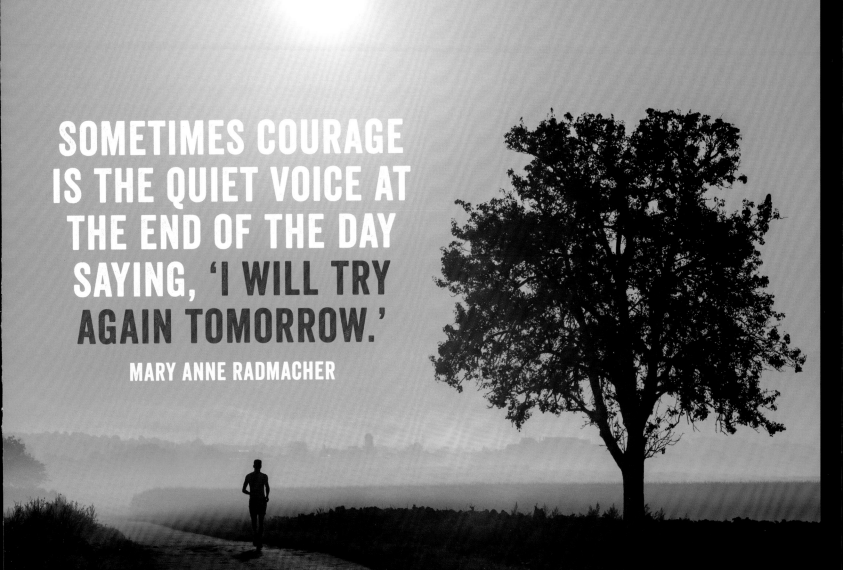

SOMETIMES COURAGE IS THE QUIET VOICE AT THE END OF THE DAY SAYING, 'I WILL TRY AGAIN TOMORROW.'

MARY ANNE RADMACHER

ACKNOWLEDGEMENTS

First and foremost, thanks go to all of the photographers for providing such brilliant photos – it couldn't have been done without your support. Special thanks go to the Uplace-BMC Pro Triathlon athletes who feature in the book.

PHOTO CREDITS

(In Alphabetical Order)

Alberto Loyo/Shutterstock

Andre Klopper/Shutterstock

Angela Aladro Mella/Shutterstock

Annette Shaff/Shutterstock

Bert Stephani

Bluecrayola/Shutterstock

Bostjan Uran/Shutterstock

Carsten Medom Madsen/Shutterstock

Christian Siebert

Dirima/Shutterstock

Ditty_About_Summer/Shutterstock

Dudarev Mikhail/Shutterstock

Efecreata Media Group/Shutterstock

Epicstockmedia/Shutterstock

H. Kopp-Delaney

Halfpoint/Shutterstock

I T A L O/Shutterstock

Jaromir Chalabala/Shutterstock

Jbor/Shutterstock

Jcsmilly/Shutterstock

Laurence Bond

Leena Robinson/Shutterstock

Maridav/Shutterstock

Martin Good/Shutterstock

Maxisport/Shutterstock

Mervin Lei

Msgrafixx/Shutterstock

Photosani/Shutterstock

Rena Schild/Shutterstock

Reto Frutig

Rihardzz/Shutterstock

S. Pytel/Shutterstock

Sainthorant Daniel/Shutterstock

Sam Smith (www.flickr.com/photos/sam-smith)

Sayam Trirattanapaiboon/Shutterstock

Stefan Holm/Shutterstock

Stemack/Shutterstock

Tami Freed/Shutterstock

Tomas Picka/Shutterstock

Warren Goldswain/Shutterstock

Wavebreakmedia/Shutterstock

Yanlev/Shutterstock

BIKE PORN

VOLUME 1

CHRIS NAYLOR

BIKE PORN
VOLUME 1

Chris Naylor

£14.99
Hardback
ISBN: 978-1-84953-481-9

All bikes are beautiful, but some are downright sexy.

BIKE PORN brings together stunning photographs of some of the most seductive and tantalising bikes ever made, from the slickest single-speeds to the most teched-out racing machines and beyond, captured in all their finely crafted glory.

If you're interested in finding out more about our books, find us on Facebook at **SUMMERSDALE PUBLISHERS** and follow us on Twitter at **@SUMMERSDALE**.

WWW.SUMMERSDALE.COM